SAINT JOHN
THE BAPTIST

SAINT JOHN THE BAPTIST

by

J.B. Midgley

The Saint Austin Press
296 Brockley Road, London, SE4 2RA
Anno MMI

The Saint Austin Press
296 Brockley Road, London, SE4 2RA

Tel 020 8692 6009
Fax 020 8469 3609
email: books@saintaustin.org
internet: www.saintaustin.org

ISBN 1 901157 37 7

Designed and printed by NEWTON Design & Print, London, UK
http://www.newtondp.co.uk

CONTENTS

DEDICATION

✣

In memory of
Brother Edwin Bannon, FSC.

Preface from the Right Revd. Peter Smith, Bishop of East Anglia

In Luke's Gospel, the story of the birth of John the Baptist is interwoven with the story of the birth of Jesus. When the birth of John was announced by the angel Gabriel, his father, Zechariah, was struck dumb because of his disbelief. But when John was born, Zechariah's speech was restored. Filled with the Holy Spirit he proclaimed the *Benedictus*, the great hymn of praise which is used daily in the Liturgy of the Hours. "And you, little child, shall be called Prophet of the Most High, you will go before the Lord to prepare the way for him."

John is a fascinating figure who stands between the Old and New Testament periods, and who stands between Jesus' hidden life and his public ministry. He is a charismatic figure whose rigorous preaching of baptism and repentance dominates the beginning of the Gospel. Jesus himself held John in great regard and refers to him as "more than a prophet."

In his portrayal of this mighty figure, Barry Midgley provides a stimulating account of the life and background of John the Baptist. We learn a little more about this extraordinary "forerunner" of Jesus and we are led into a knowledge of some of the factors which formed this remarkable man and made him so attractive as to command the respect of the ordinary people of his time. He was the great witness who came "to speak for the light" - Jesus the light of the world. We too can profit from knowing him a little better, that he may lead us too to a greater knowledge and love of the one Saviour, Jesus Christ.

Bishop of East Anglia

St John the Baptist from a painting by Mantegna

"Jesus began to talk to the people about John. What did you go out into the wilderness to see? A reed shaken by the breeze?...To see a prophet? Yes, I tell you and much more than a prophet: he is the one of whom Scripture says: Look, I am going to send my messenger before you. I tell you solemnly, of all the children born of women, a greater than John the Baptist has never been..." (Matthew 11:7-11).

Introduction

During the Advent season, Christians relive the expectation of the Messiah's arrival in the person of Jesus Christ. It is a time when the Church directs our attention to the prophetic mission of Saint John the Baptist who was chosen by God to preach a baptism of repentance for the forgiveness of sins so that the world should be prepared for an event of eternal immensity.

We know that God made Man will return in glory at the Last Day but, in the meantime, He comes in ways which are not always recognised: in the person of the poor, the afflicted, the sorrowing, the stranger, the captive, the alienated. John's call to prepare a way for the Lord is always contemporary and his intercession continues to help our human hearts welcome God's reign of justice, peace and truth.

Every year we share a regret that, apart from his two Feasts, a powerful friend and advocate has not been remembered as he deserves. In this first year of a new millennium, these pages attempt to make some amends.

The Baptism of the Lord, 2001   J.B.Midgley,
                                             Downham Market.

Parmigianino's Virgin and Child with Ss John the Baptist and Jerome. (Courtesy of the Trustees of the National Gallery.)

CHAPTER ONE
Three of John's predecessors

In God's eternal present moment, when "a day can mean a thousand years and a thousand years is like a day" (2 Peter 3:8), the divine inspiration of the Old Testament joins the New in the expression of the Father's single plan of salvation and the consolation of His children.

Elijah

An early indication of John the Baptist's place in salvation history comes with Elijah, a prophet who "arose like a fire and his word burned like a sword", (Ecclesiasticus 48:1), during the unedifying reigns of Ahab and his son, Ahaziah, in the northern kingdom of Israel BC 874-852. It was a time when the nation enjoyed great prosperity but when, at the same time, Israel's faith was severely tested. Ahab's pleasure-seeking and forceful wife, Jezebel, was devoted to the pagan god Baal and, to promote an idolatrous fertility cult, built a temple which was served by four hundred priests maintained at her own expense. She attempted to ensure the success of her venture by slaughtering God's prophets and ruthlessly persecuting the Israelites.

The Book of Kings portrays Elijah as a man of prayer, fierce determination and dauntless courage. Despite the likelihood of dire consequences, he did not hesitate to confront Ahab and condemn his misdeeds and the excesses of his queen who then pursued him with such animosity that he had to take refuge in the wilderness. His steadfastness was rewarded when Ahab experienced a change of heart for the better, perhaps stimulated by a three-year drought which God had sent to emphasise His prophet's warnings. When Jezebel remained implacable Elijah, finding himself the sole surviving voice, went on a difficult journey to find God on Sinai's mountain of Horeb and, having arrived, shouted for help. In answer God revealed Himself and restored the prophet's confidence with encouragement to persevere in the battle against idolatry. Elijah built an altar on Mount Carmel so that he might offer a bull in sacrifice to the Lord and challenged Jezebel's "prophets of Baal" to do likewise. God sent down fire from heaven to consume his acceptable sacrifice but Baal showed no such favour! His prophets were exposed as fraudsters and the faith of Israel was saved. Ahab and Jezebel were similarly disappointed, the king being killed in a revolution and his queen thrown from a window to her death by the supporters of Jehu. (1 Kings 18, 19, 21; 2 Kings 16).

Elijah's mission was sustained by a life of prayer, self denial and a total trust in God. When his task was complete and God sent a chariot of fire through the clouds to convey him to heaven, he comforted Elisha, his disciple and successor, telling him that "the Lord is taking me only as far as the Jordan." (2 Kings 2:1-13). So it was that the Jews confidently expected the prophet to return and be seen on Jordan's banks.

The Carmelites have a great devotion to Elijah and some of their writers contend that he founded their Order which is, in their opinion, the oldest in the Church. Another view is that it was not formally established until the thirteenth century but had, indeed, evolved from the association of hermits who, inspired by Elijah, lived in caves on the western slopes of Mount Carmel, the scene of Baal's embarrassment. This is still the location of his shrine and the Carmelites keep his Feast on July 20th, four days after that of Our Lady of Mount Carmel.

Isaiah

Isaiah, BC 740-700, the greatest of the Hebrew prophets, was also a consummate statesman who saved Jerusalem from the siege of the Assyrians. When he was favoured with a vision in the Temple, he was given a heightened awareness of God's holiness, love and power which extends beyond Israel to every person of every nation for He is the Lord of all whose mercy rests on all He has created. (Isaiah 6:1-7). As prophet of the Incarnation he speaks of a herald who will announce a new Exodus which, like the liberation from Egypt, will manifest God's glory and much more because this time it is God's very own Son who will bring deliverance by becoming Man. Straight and level ways must be prepared to welcome such a King and Conqueror. "A voice cries, 'Prepare, in the wilderness, a way for the Lord. Make a straight highway for our God across the desert. Let every valley be filled in, every mountain and hill be laid low, let every cliff become a plain and the ridge a valley; then the glory of the Lord shall be revealed and all mankind shall see it.'" (Isaiah 40: 1-5).

The herald will alert the cities of Juda to God's return with His exiled people. "Go up to a high mountain joyful messenger to Jerusalem. Shout with fear, say to the towns of juda, 'Here is your God; here is the Lord coming with power, His arm sustaining all things to Him. He is like a shepherd leading His flock, gathering lambs in His arms, holding them against His breast and leading to their rest the mother ewes." (40:9-11). Isaiah's tender simile points to Jesus the Good Shepherd whose boundless compassion spares no effort to recover even a single wanderer from His universal flock. The straggler has yet to experience the joy of reunion with Christ and, at one time or another, every soul awaits the reconciliation He brings.

Isaiah reminds us that it is God Himself who decides upon the names of the prophets. "The Lord called me before I was born, from my mother's womb He pronounced my name. He made my mouth a sharp sword...He has formed me in the womb to be His servant, to bring Jacob back to Him, to gather Israel to Him." (49:1-6). Later, when

Gabriel is sent by God to tell Zechariah that he and his wife, Elizabeth, are to be blessed with a son, it is also with an instruction that the boy is to be called John which means "God is gracious".

The prophet's messages that God would comfort His people were understood by the Jews to mean that they could expect the Messiah, the Anointed One who would free them from the yoke of foreign oppression. It is, however, the baptism brought by John which will initiate their liberation by the Lamb of God whom he will identify. When Jesus comes to fulfil the Messianic prophecies, He will explain that His Kingdom, to which everyone is an heir, is not of this world and that He is a King who will rule by serving others.

Malachi

John links the Old Testament to the New, representing the one while introducing the other. Malachi, his immediate predecessor, articulates God's promise of Elijah's return to open people's hearts so that they are disposed to welcome the Messiah. "Know that I am going to send you Elijah, the prophet, before my day comes, that great and terrible day. He shall turn the hearts of fathers towards their children and the hearts of children towards their fathers...(Malachi 4:6).

He possessed the great courage of a prophet and denounced corrupt behaviour wherever he found it either in the priesthood or among the people and seized every opportunity to recommend a better way of life.

ST JOHN THE BAPTIST

He emphasised the necessity of appropriate preparation for God's personal arrival on earth, His entry into time which would bring a purer worship among the gentiles to replace that of the Old Testament. Even a note of excitement can be detected as the Incarnation draws near. "Look I am going to send my messenger to prepare a way before me. And the Lord you are seeking will suddenly enter the Temple and the Angel of the Covenant whom you are longing for, Yes He is coming."

(Malachi 3:1).

The Prophecy of Malachi concludes with God's wish that the Law which he gave to his servant Moses should not be forgotten for it is within the framework of the Mosaic dispensation that John's miraculous conception will be announced. An angel will bring news of God's plan to a Levitical priest in the temple at Jerusalem where the lamb is sacrificed and he will draw together the themes introduced by Elijah, Isaiah and Malachi. "He John, will bring back many of the sons of Israel to the Lord their God. With the spirit and power of Elijah he will go before Him to turn the hearts of fathers towards their children." (Luke 1:17). The Law was given to Moses and now grace and truth are come through Jesus Christ. (Cf John 1:17).

From Overbeck's 'The naming of St. John the Baptist'

CHAPTER TWO

The parents of John the Baptist

Saint Luke (1:1-25) introduces us to an admirable Jewish couple, the priest Zechariah and his wife Elizabeth who, in their fidelity to the Mosaic Law, meet with God's approval and offer a happy contrast to those who so disappointed the prophets of old. In prayer and patient service they wait for God to deliver His people even though they do not know how or when this might come to pass. That they are childless is a cause of great sadness and they might have been the object of derision because the first commandment for the Jews was to go forth and multiply, fill the earth and subdue it.

The Jewish Priesthood

Zechariah was a priest of the family of Abia, one of twenty-four sacerdotal families into which the descendants of Aaron were divided to facilitate the rotation of duties in the Temple. The sacred offices were hereditary and a man became a priest by being of the tribe of Levi and the priestly vocation was transmitted, therefore, from father to son. It is hardly surprising that the Jewish priesthood was numerous and the historian, Flavius Josephus, estimated that in Zechariah's time there were about twenty thousand non-celibate priests serving a population of some five million.

Because they were so many, Jewish priests were required to officiate in the Temple for only one week twice a year but, even then, numbers demanded that major ministrations had to be allocated by the drawing of lots. Each day, four main sacerdotal responsibilities were assigned: the offering of the burnt sacrifice at morning and evening; the care of the seven-branch candlestick in the ante-chamber to the Holy of Holies; the weekly renewal of the twelve ceremonial loaves placed on a golden table in the ante-chamber and representing the twelve tribes of Israel. Then there was the most cherished task of all, to burn fragrant incense on the Golden Altar in the Lord's sanctuary at the appropriate hour every day before the lamb was sacrificed and while the people prayed outside. This was such an honoured responsibility that only once in his lifetime might a priest be allowed to offer the incense and, having done so, was ineligible to participate in the future drawing of that particular lot.

The Altar of Incense

Throughout his life as a priest, Zechariah had drawn lots at first light for the offering of incense. Now that he was old perhaps he had resigned himself to the fact that the privilege was not to be his, just as his hopes of becoming a father had likewise evaporated. His joy can be imagined when, at long last, fortune smiled on him and, dressed in the ceremonial white robe, he processed to perform the greatest act of his priesthood. Holding the golden saucer of incense, he went behind the sumptuous tapestry which hung before the Holy Place and then stepped into the sanctuary itself. He approached the Altar and sprinkled the incense on the live coals. As the fragrance ascended, he lifted his eyes to Heaven and saw the brilliance of an Angel.

Gabriel brings news of John's conception

Although they had a most devoted and close relationship with God, the Jewish people were not entirely enthusiastic about heavenly visions which they thought might well indicate a premature, if not imminent departure from this earthly life. Zechariah, already emotionally charged by the ritual, was thoroughly alarmed as Gabriel spoke, "Your prayer has been heard and your wife Elizabeth is going to give you a son and you must name him John."

Now during the offering of the incense it was customary for priest and people to pray for the coming of the Messiah and the redemption of Israel but it would be understandable if, on this occasion, the celebrant had reminded God about his request for a son. The patient loyalty of Zechariah and Elizabeth is rewarded with the momentous news that not only are they to be parents but that their child is to prepare the way for the Messiah whose day he will declare. Zechariah is nonplussed and asks, "How is this going to happen? Elizabeth and I are old." The sign which Gabriel gives him could not be more convincing because, literally, he is left speechless for having doubts about God's message and its promise. Incidentally, Saint Luke hints that he may also have become deaf because when the time comes for him to give his son a name, the assembled relatives had to make signals to him. (Luke 1:62).

It should be remembered that names were particularly important to the people of Israel and were usually linked to family tradition, special circumstances and the belief that choice of name influenced the development of character. So it is that , with wonderful accuracy, 'Zechariah' means 'God has remembered', Elizabeth', 'God has promised' and John, as we know, 'God is gracious'. The thoughts suggested by these names will be echoed in Mary's 'Magnificat', Zechariah's 'Benedictus' and Simeon's 'Nunc Dimittis', three canticles which embrace phrases from the Mosaic Law, the Prophets and the Psalms, all of which are centred upon Christ. He Himself, on the road to Emmaus with two disciples after His Resurrection, will explain how the Law, the Prophets and the Psalms are fulfilled in Him and how names preserve the continuity between events past, present and to come.

When Zechariah asked Gabriel for some confirmation it was not because he had doubts about God's power but because he wondered whether God loved him enough to this wonderful thing for him. Sometimes we find that our trust in God can be limited and specific rather than uncompromising and complete. A prayer of petition which lacks such trust may be directed more to God's performance than to His word. Unless there is attachment to the Divine Will, the petitioner could ask for something while suspecting that God might prefer otherwise and that it is *His* will which will be done. Faith does not eliminate life's anxieties but it gives life to the hope which surrounds circumstances and which puts the Divine Will before all else. We are more favoured than Zechariah because we, in the New Covenant, have been given the further assurances of God's love which Christ has brought.

Elizabeth

The many women who adorn the pages of the Gospel vary in age from Anna, the prophetess at Jesus' Presentation in the Temple, to the little daughter of Jairus; in virtue from Mary, the peerless Mother of God, to the widely experienced lady from Samaria; in personality from Mary Magdalen to the formidable portress who gives Peter such a hard time on the first Maundy Thursday evening. Of them all, Elizabeth is the chronological first, the dutiful wife of Zechariah and the mother of the Messiah's herald and, through her relationship to Jesus and Mary is a member of history's central family. The precise degree of blood relationship to Mary is not known. Some have suggested they were first cousins but, in view of the obvious age gap, it is more likely that Elizabeth was Mary's aunt.

She must have been taken aback when her husband arrived home from his Temple duties unable to say a word and had to write down the details of his extraordinary experience but, even with the humiliation of sterility, her trust in God has never wavered. Perhaps her maternal longing predisposed her to accept Gabriel's news more readily than her husband. Certainly, she conceived shortly afterwards and thanked God for His great goodness (Luke 1:25), no doubt recalling Isaiah's "Shout for joy you barren women who bore no children. Break into cries of joy and gladness you who were never in labour...Do not be afraid, you will not be put to shame; do not be dismayed, you will not be disgraced." (54:1-10). God has, indeed, been faithful to His promise and has an even more exalted moment in store for her.

Mary visits Elizabeth

Meanwhile God and His messenger have been busily engaged elsewhere, informing another Mother about another Infant. Gabriel tells Mary that she has conceived by the power of the Holy Spirit and is to be the Mother of the Most High. He gives her the happy news about Elizabeth as an assurance that nothing is beyond God's power. Without the slightest doubt, she immediately sets out from Nazareth, not to verify the sign but to help her elderly relative in her pregnancy. Elizabeth and Zechariah lived in a town in the hill country of Judaea, possibly Ain Karim five miles from Jerusalem, or the sacerdotal town of Hebron a little farther distant but still convenient for the Temple. In either case, for a young girl it was a demanding journey of about sixty miles and one likes to think that Joachim and Anne accompanied their daughter and made it a family occasion.

Nazareth, in the unfashionable province of Galilee, was a town of about one hundred and fifty inhabitants and so obscure that it attracted some ridicule. "Can anything good come out of Nazareth?" asked Nathaniel, an early disciple of Jesus. (John 1:46). From this unpromising location God chose His plan of action to take shape when He asked Mary to exceed perceived boundaries of propriety and risk her reputation in an apparently inexplicable motherhood.

John's first Meeting with the Messiah

After her unhesitating 'Fiat', Mary wanted to help Elizabeth during a difficult and anxious time and share a joy as great as it was unexpected. The Holy Spirit uses her kindness to inspire Elizabeth and her unborn son who, as Mary embraces his mother, leaps for joy in early recognition of the Saviour now in Mary's womb.

> *"Ere long, that Holy Child she bore*
> *By Gabriel's message named before,*
> *Whom, yet unborn, with eager pride*
> *The swift forerunner prophesied."*
>
> *(Hymn, Liturgy of the Hours, The Nativity)*

The Incarnate Word sanctifies John and he who is to baptise and preach repentance will be cleansed from original sin and, in the opinion of the Fathers of the Church, have full possession of the use of reason. After Jesus and Mary, therefore, he alone has his nativity celebrated by the Church.

Elizabeth proclaims, "Blessed art thou among women and blessed is the fruit of thy womb," and then wonders, "Why should I be honoured with a visit from the mother of my Lord?" It is more an answer than a question for now she is aware of the Messiah's presence and blesses Mary's unhesitating belief in God's promise. "Blessed is she who believed that the promise made her by the Lord would be fulfilled." Poor Zechariah can still say nothing. There is a reminder here of Sarah, Abraham's wife and mother of Isaac who, despite her age, conceived because "she believed that He who made the promise would be faithful to it." (Genesis 15:1-6 and cf Hebrews 11:8-12).

To Elizabeth is due thanks for that part of the 'Hail Mary' which follows Gabriel's salutation and, therefore, her contribution to the Holy Rosary. Furthermore, her greeting prompted Mary's 'Magnificat', that profound prayer which summarises God's revelation in the Old Testament and describes how eagerly His people waited for His action in their lives. "There is no need to congratulate me,'" replies Mary. "It is all the Lord's doing and I am fortunate that He has been so gracious in noticing someone so insignificant." (Luke 1:39-55). Officialdom may fail but the humble will recognise the entry of the Promised Deliverer into human history.

ST JOHN THE BAPTIST

The Lord whose arrival Elizabeth recognises and welcomes became Man for everyone without exception and He distances Himself from no one. He will work as a carpenter in a small town, live among the poor, befriend unfragrant fishermen, choose a despised tax-collector as an Apostle and Evangelist, commend the tiny offering of a poor widow, make time for children, rescue an adultress, sanctify a lady of unconventional virtue and sing the praises of an imprisoned John the Baptist.. Elizabeth understood that the Incarnation is for all God's children, the living temples of the Holy Spirit and the heirs to the Kingdom of Heaven. Each one is God's direct handiwork, made in His own image and no-one can judge who most accurately reflects that image.

CHAPTER THREE

John's early life

"There was a man sent from God whose name was John and he was filled with the Holy Spirit while still in his mother's womb by Christ Himself whom the Virgin Mary had just conceived. Her visit to Elizabeth was a visit from God to His people." (*Catechism of the Catholic Church*, 717).

John is a child promised by God and given to elderly parents as Isaac had been to Abraham and Sarah. His expected birth had been announced by the angel of the Lord in the sanctuary itself during solemn worship as befits the son of a priest and, like Samuel, he will be dedicated to God. The presence of the Holy Spirit in the child is the indication of prophetic gifts and his mission has been defined by Gabriel in the terms used by Malachi to foretell Elijah's return. He is to preach national reconciliation and revive the holy customs of the past. "He shall go before the Lord's face in the spirit and power of Elijah." (Malachi 3:1; 4:5-6).

During her pregnancy Elizabeth "kept to herself" not through embarrassment but because, at her age, her condition might give rise to ill-judged comment. There were divine secrets here which she and Mary shared with joy, understanding and mutual encouragement. It is highly unlikely that Mary would have left Elizabeth before the baby was born so it may be assumed that she was one of the "neighbours and relations" who celebrated the birth and, eight days later, attended the circumcision. In this case she would have witnessed the remarkable restoration of Zechariah's speech when he named his son "God is gracious" and listened as his 'Benedictus' complemented her 'Magnificat'.

John's circumcision

The Gospel narrative conveys the joy with which the Jewish people celebrated the religious ceremony which admits a boy to spiritual communion with Israel and a share in God's promise to the Patriarchs. Circumcision is the deed of contract between God and the boy who embraces His Law with all its privileges and responsibilities. "God said to Abraham... 'Now this is my covenant which you are to maintain between myself and you and your descendants after you: all your males must be circumcised...and this shall be the sign of the covenant between myself and you.' " (Genesis 17:9-11).

The 'Benedictus' (Luke 1:68-79)

"The tongues of the dumb shall sing for joy." (Isaiah 35:6). Nine months have passed since Zechariah was last able to speak. Then, at the sacrifice of incense, he had offered the ritual prayer of priest and people which incorporated the eighteen benedictions which summarised the hopes of Israel. When, in obedience to God, he names his son John, his speech surges back in a hymn of praise which echoes the Judaeic prayers and acknowledges that God has remembered, promised and is gracious in salvation. As the 'Magnificat' harmonises with Mary's character, so does the 'Benedictus' with Zechariah's and both embrace the intentions of the Old Covenant now reaching fulfilment. To express its continuing joy in the Saviour, the Church includes these canticles in its daily Liturgy of the Hours.

"Blessed be the Lord God of Israel. He has visited His people and redeemed them. He has raised up for us a mighty Saviour in the House of David His servant, as He promised by the lips of holy men, those who were his prophets from of old; a Saviour who would free us from our foes, from the hands of all who hate us. So, His love for our fathers is fulfilled and His holy covenant remembered." The "visiting of His people" by God is a phrase often used to describe His coming to help, judge, show mercy, pardon and save. Now, Zechariah is able to join his wife in voicing his homage to Mary's Child. The name of David's descendant is 'Jesus' which means 'Yahweh is salvation' and He is the mighty Saviour who delivers us from the enmity of sin and death. The 'holy covenant' is that made between God and Abraham on whom He showered blessings in reward for obedience and promised that his offspring, that is every man and woman God creates, "as many as the stars of heaven", would overcome their foes and rejoice in being his descendants.

Zechariah blesses God for the preparatory work of salvation which will be undertaken by his own son John, the ultimate prophet who is to bring all prophecy to its triumphant conclusion. "As for you little child, you shall be called the prophet of God the Most High. You shall go ahead of the Lord to prepare His ways before Him, to make known to his people their salvation through forgiveness of all their sins: the loving kindness of the heart of our God who visits us like the dawn from on high. He will give light to those in darkness, those who dwell in the shadow of death and guide us into the way of peace."

John's father has recalled Malachi's promise, on God's behalf, of a new Elijah who would bring the message that the way must be prepared for the angel of the New Covenant. (Malachi 3:1; 4:2). Some of the people were later to think that it was Jesus Himself who was the Elijah coming to announce God's great and terrible day. He will correct their thinking by confirming that it is John to whom the prophecies of the Old Law point as the new Elijah coming to see that all is as it should be. (Matthew 3:21; Mark 9:2).

Of Elizabeth and Zechariah no more is heard. They disappear from the Gospel pages but there is a tradition in the Eastern Church, supported by Saint Basil and Saint Cyril, that Zechariah was martyred in the Temple he had served with such distinction at the command of Herod the Great. The Roman Martyrology says nothing about this except that John's splendid parents are honoured together as saints on their Feastday of November 5th. They offer a model of marriage to an age when the Sacrament which gives men and women a share in God's work of creation might be overlooked. Later their son will meet another couple whose views on marriage are less exemplary.

A hidden life

"Meanwhile, the child grew up and his spirit matured. And he lived in the wilderness until the day he appeared openly to Israel." (Luke 1:80). This observation will not be the only example of Saint Luke's ability to describe development over a long period in a few words as we see when he tells us of Jesus' hidden life after His Presentation in the Temple and His being found there twelve years later. (Luke 2:40;52).

The "spirit" is that divine spirit which came to John while he was still in his mother's womb, brought him the prophetic gifts and, later, will lead him to the desert. We do not know how old John was when he left the family home but, clearly, he made no claim to the priesthood which was his by right of birth and we can only wonder at the sacrifice of his parents in relinquishing their beloved child to the destiny to which God called him. He is the herald of Christ who is of the House of David, not of Aaron. The Old Law and its Temple was drawing to its conclusion. John intended to practice what he would preach through a penitential life of prayer, untouched by sin or the world. For the time being, he emulated the sons of Rahab who, in earlier times, had drawn Israel's attention to the example of the Patriarchs by remaining faithful to the desert life. "We have meticulously obeyed the orders of our ancestor Jonadab, son of Rechab, never drinking wine ourselves...nor building houses to live in...and living in tents." (Jeremiah 35:6).

John and the Essenes

Because they have been associated with John's life, a word about the Essenes may be appropriate. Like the Pharisees and Saducees they flourished in Palestine from the middle of the second century BC until the Roman conquest in AD 70. Though Jewish and Roman writers like Josephus and Pliny refer to them, oddly enough they are not mentioned in the New Testament. Yet, throughout Judaea, groups of these men withdrew from society to prepare for the coming of God's Kingdom and lived a community life of prayer,self-denial, labour and the study of the sacred scriptures. Pliny tells of one such community which settled near the shores of the Dead Sea and, in all probability, this included the scribes of the Qumran Scrolls which were discovered in 1947 and which reveal information about Essene philosophy and way of life. They ate frugally, abstained from strong drink, practised celibacy and common ownership of goods, conducted ritual cleansing with water and were led by a priest who was given the title of "Teacher of Righteousness". They were concerned that the Jews may have become lukewarm in their religious observance and so they distanced themselves from worship in the Temple though they were faithful in contributing to its maintenance.

On the question of whether or not John was an Essene scholarship is divided but there is reasoned consensus that he must have been very aware of a group whose piety and devoted observance coincided with the values bequeathed to him by his parents. . It is likely that he chose the Judaean Desert for his dwelling, the mountainous region flanking the Dead sea and the river Jordan where he would be able to conduct his ministry of baptism and where caves offering shelter to a hermit abounded. Since Qumran is in the same vicinity, John could hardly have avoided some contact with the monastic community and there is some reason to believe that Zechariah may have entrusted his young son to its care and that John spent some time as a postulant or novice before the Spirit led him to the wilderness. Prophets seldom emerge without some experience and education. The Scrolls show that the Essenes had a great admiration for Isaiah and studied his prophecies with great attention. Perhaps they inspired John's own understanding of the prophet and his promise of the voice in the wilderness which would summon Jewry to construct a straight highway in the desert for God's arrival and to announce the greatest news ever, that Salvation is here.

Appearance, dress and diet

It is probable that John had taken the vow of a Nazarite, avoiding alcohol and wearing his hair long as a sign of his separation to the Lord like Samson and Samuel before him.(Judges 13:5). Such appearance is evocative of the prophet Zechariah who insisted, "I am no prophet; I am a peasant; the land has been my living since I was a boy. (Zechariah 13:4). More significantly perhaps, John's clothing replicates Elijah's: a coat of animal hair and a loin cloth made of skin. (2 Kings 1:8). From the Gospel we know that his staple food was locusts and wild honey. The Essenes ate these winged, easily caught insects either boiled or roasted, a prudent practice still adopted by the Bedouin peoples. The wild honey could have been the edible tree-gum which was plentiful on the banks of the Jordan.

CHAPTER FOUR

John's public life

According to Saint Luke, John began his ministry, preaching in the wilderness of Judaea, about 27 AD in the fifteenth year of the reign of the Emperor Tiberius. We have Josephus' description of him as an ascetic who quickly won popularity and respect among the Jews as he announced his baptism and penitential message in the mountainous district east of the Jerusalem-Hebron road. "In those days there appeared among the Jews, a man in strange garments who called them to liberty saying, 'God has sent me that I should show you the way of the Law in which you will free yourselves from many tyrants, and no mortal will ever ride over you, only the Most High who has sent me.' And all Jerusalem followed him. And he did nothing to them but that he dipped them in the River Jordan and then dismissed them, exhorting them that they should cease from evil works." (Antiquities Bk 2, Ch vii).

Preparing the way

The exhortation to a change of heart which attracted such a considerable following and caught the interest of Josephus was, in other words, a call to the essential disposition to receive the divine gift of the Kingdom of God which is on the point of arrival. The Messianic prophecies had promised such a realm and God's rule, so these were not unexpected phenomena but the supernatural climax of the Divine Plan which had been revealed and developed throughout Israel's history. John is to follow Elijah, his prophetic prototype, in a life of prayer, self-denial, trust in God and courage in the face of suffering. It is not surprising that some assumed he must be Elijah returned.

All four Evangelists recognise him as the realisation of the prophetic vision, Mark even opening his text with Isaiah's forecast of the promised messenger and later Jesus Himself at His Transfiguration will confirm "' I tell you that Elijah has already' come and they did not recognise him and treated him as they pleased and the Son of Man will suffer similarly at their hands.' The disciples understood that He had been speaking of John the Baptist." (Matthew 17:9-13).

John was not the only itinerant prophet seeking to initiate a new society but, unlike some others, he had no interest in making a name for himself, nor did he claim to be the Deliverer come to eradicate political and social injustice. He insisted he was only a messenger, a voice bringing happy news of a different kind of kingdom altogether. Since they were familiar with the scriptures, the Jews had come to expect a messenger like Elijah and now in John they saw the very person. They were well aware of the conclusions reached by the prophets that, despite their being chosen by God for a special relationship with Him, they were not particularly ready to meet with Him or if His coming was to have any influence in their lives. They had wearied him with their hardness of heart and His arrival might well bring to the privileged a judgment all the more severe. John warned of One "who would chop down trees that yield no fruit and burn chaff away from the wheat." (Luke 3:7-17). God judges all His people with nothing but fairness but John advised groups like the Pharisees and the Saducees not to delude themselves that the Romans were necessarily the first in line for chastisement.

Pharisees and Saducees

The Pharisees or "the separated ones" were devoted to the details of the written Law, its accompanying traditions and the strict observance of the priestly code. As professional holy men they wielded much influence though they had no official religious or political position in the state. The Saducees, the "sons of Zadok", represented the priestly line appointed by David to lead the chant in the Temple of the Lord after the Ark of the Covenant came to be housed there. (1 Chronicles 6:8-15). They were traditionalists who did not believe in a life after death and, although they counted the High Priest and members of the priestly families among their number, they did not enjoy much popularity. Both groups had an interest in the Sanhedrin, the Jewish Governing Body which included the High Priests. The Pharisees manipulated events through the Scribes who had made themselves indispensable as teachers and interpreters of the Law. The Saducees were not particularly bothered about which regime held sway in the land as long as their own position was secure and the Pharisees, although they loathed the occupying power, carefully refrained from displaying any nationalistic tendencies.

Neither group could afford to ignore John's popularity. It seems that some of the Pharisees had a genuine interest in his religious movement but there was a general anxiety that it could take a political turn to their disadvantage. John knew very well that they came to his baptisms more as spies than as disciples and that, "like a brood of vipers", their motives were subtle and venomous. Even so, they still had time to repent and he would not deny them the chance to respond to his theme of evading wrath and an unfavourable Messianic judgment. (Matthew 3:7-12).

Repentance

"Repent for the Kingdom of Heaven is near. Prepare the way of the Lord, make His paths straight." (Matthew 3:2-3).

The new Elijah's message is that repentance is not just a matter of being sorry or making one's conscience comfortable for the time being. It is more an interior attitude which contemplates God's holiness and His integrity and contrasts these with sinfulness. John saw repentance as a fundamental turning away from sin, a conversion of heart and behaviour which responds to the salvation the Messiah brings. There is an accompanying joy in God's mercy and a sense of freedom from the shackles of guilt which are the bequests of sin. Clearing paths, making them straight, levelling mountains and valleys is a tall order. We can no more repent of ourselves than we can make ourselves holy but we can be sure that the Holy Spirit who gives us the desire to repent, to become holy, will always be there, helping us to become so.

The repentance which John encourages is related to the Sacrament of Baptism which, in our own day, we are able to understand and appreciate with the help of the Church and her teaching: the bath which purifies, justifies and sanctifies, when we put on Christ and receive the Holy Spirit who inspires our desire to draw close to God and conform our lives more to the likeness of His Son. The gifts brought by Baptism remain constant, assisting a recognition of the difference between the life we lead now and the Divine Life we are destined to share so that the barriers we erect between ourselves and God, and between each other, can be taken down. Grace is forthcoming so that we can welcome the pardon Christ brings and hearts of stone become hearts of flesh. Most importantly, we receive grace to forgive ourselves for the devil, the real enemy of whom the prophets spoke and from whose tyranny we are freed, tries to persuade us that we are too far gone for a change of heart!

God wills to share His own wisdom with us, so that we are at one with Him and our bruised integrity is healed. "Darkness will not blind us to the vision of wisdom...a new heaven and a new earth where righteousness will be at home." Such a reformation of life yields the appropriate fruit identified by John (Matthew 3:8) which gives glory to God by obedience to His commandments and "by loving one another deeply from the heart", because in Baptism "we have been born anew...of imperishable seed." (1 Peter 1:22-23).

CHAPTER FIVE

John baptises

Most Jews would have been familiar with the concept of baptism because it was used to admit gentiles to Judaeism and, as already noticed, the Essenes used ritual washing to encourage moral and religious purity. The New Testament and Josephus describe John's baptism as a call to put lives in order prior to the Messiah's arrival and those willing to accept such a challenge showed their commitment by being washed in the cleansing waters of the Jordan near Jericho. Accepting John's baptism was an acknowledgement of belief that the Kingdom of God was close at hand with a determination to admit and remedy faults.

John was careful to explain that his baptism and exhortation to repentance was only a preparation for the Baptism in the Holy Spirit which the Messiah would bring. It illustrated a transition from the limited rite of the Jewish ceremonial bath, intended to cleanse gentile defilement, to the efficacious, sacramental Baptism in Christ, and a progression from the Law to the Gospel. It did not make people Christians but prepared them for an interior, sacramental re-birth.

John's counsels were very much in accord with those of Christ: that a penitential preparation for a "Kingdom of righteousness, peace and joy in the Holy Spirit" (Romans 14:17) brings a change in disposition symbolised not just by washing but by a new life. Before He left His Apostles at His Ascension, Christ reminded them that John baptised with water but they would be baptised with the Holy Spirit. Such a Baptism is the outpouring of the gifts of grace not merely in the Sacrament but in the entire economy of salvation. "For I will pour out water on the thirsty soil, my Spirit on your descendants...my blessing on your children." (Isaiah 44:3).

John baptises Jesus

When he had been preaching and baptising for about six months, John sensed that some of the Jews were beginning to give him the kind of reverence to which he was not entitled. He had to repeat that he baptised only with water while there was One coming to baptise in the Holy Spirit who was so worthy of true reverence that he was not worthy to perform the most menial task of untying His sandal. The Jews, however, were not to easily deflected and sent an embassy of priests and Levites to ask John outright if he were one of the expected figures who would announce the Day of the Lord, the Messiah, Elijah or even Moses. "No", he told them. "I am just the voice in the wilderness asking you to prepare for the Lord's coming."

Righteousness

Jesus was now thirty years of age and had left Nazareth, travelling south to the district bordering the Jordan where John was baptising and calling Israel to mend its ways. When He presented Himself for baptism, John was, at first reluctant. "It is I who need baptism from You and Yet you come to me," but Jesus reassured him. "Leave it like this for the time being; it is fitting that we should do all that righteousness demands." (Matthew 3:13-15). It was Jeremiah who had promised that a Righteous Branch would issue from the House of David and his prophecy is fulfilled in Christ, the Sun of Righteousness whose dawning light dispels the darkness of sin and the shadows of death and who brings justice, not as a political enforcer but as a Servant King changing hearts as a branch bears new life.

In being baptised by John, Jesus gives his mission the greatest possible approval and accepts His own as God's suffering servant. Though sinless and without need of repentance and cleansing, He wishes to be counted among sinners. The Lamb of God who takes away all sin, is anticipating His sacrifice upon the altar of the Cross. "There is a baptism I must still receive, and how great is my distress till it is over." (Luke 12:50). Lovingly obedient to His Father's will, with John's baptism He accepts the baptism of death which saves us from the results of sin.

"The blood and water which flowed from His precious side present for us Baptism and the Eucharist, the Sacraments of new life, of being born of water and the Spirit to enter the Kingdom of God." (Catechism of the Catholic Church, 1225).

Although John did not baptise without instructing candidates, he recognised Jesus as a teacher like no other and, given the family love which characterised Mary's Visitation to Elizabeth, it is unlikely that they were total strangers to each other. In any case, we can assume from

Saint Matthew's Gospel that there had been prior conversation during which John had reached his conclusions. He certainly recognised Jesus' desire to identify Himself with the repentant sinners who would become His disciples, in whose lives He would be totally involved and whom, in the persons of the Apostles, He would commission to teach all nations and baptise them in the name of the Father, the Son and the Holy Spirit present at His own baptism.

"No sooner had He come out of the water than He saw the heavens torn apart and the Spirit, like a Dove, descending on Him and a voice came from Heaven, 'You are my Son, the Beloved. My favour rests on You." (Mark 1:9-11).

Jesus' baptism of water is followed by Baptism in the Holy Spirit who, like a Dove, brooded on the face of the waters in the first Creation. It now rests on Jesus to bring a new Creation while the Father, the Voice of Creation in the beginning, claims His Beloved Son and invests Him in His mission with Messianic dignity.

Now the Spirit leads Jesus to the desert where He fasts for forty days and nights to prepare for His encounter with Satan, the enemy of the Messianic plan. He who has no need of penance takes His share for our learning and to give the devil notice that the battle for mankind has been joined.

John points to Jesus as the Lamb of God

"Seeing Jesus coming towards him, John said, 'Look, there is the Lamb of God who takes away the sin of the world.'" (John 1:29-30).

When Abraham took his cherished son Isaac to be sacrificed in unquestioned obedience to God's instruction, the boy innocently

asked why there seemed to be no lamb for the burnt offering. His father told him that God would make provision. When God was about to deliver His people from slavery, He asked that a Passover lamb, a young male without blemish, should be offered and, in eating it, the Hebrews accepted His mercy and deliverance. When Isaiah foretold the coming of God's chosen and suffering Servant, he saw Him as One who would "Be lead out as a lamb to the slaughter."

The prologue to Saint John's G ospel connects the man sent by God whose name was John to the mystical vision at the baptism of Jesus. He announces the Victorious Light, the Sun of Justice who reveals His glory so that all may live in God through His healing light. When the Father claims Jesus as his beloved Son, John knew He was,indeed, the Messiah to be made known to the Jews and that his mission as prophetic herald was almost at an end. He points out Jesus as the "Lamb of God" and in this expression of sacred significance all the Old Testament images are completed. Jesus is the Sacrificial, Paschal Lamb without blemish offered for our sins and who, in the Eucharist, gives His flesh and blood for our spiritual food. As He did for Abraham and Isaac, God has provided the sacrifice.

In so identifying Jesus, John foretells His death and the ending of the whole sacrificial ritual of Judaeism. Everything the prophets promised has come to be and John, the last of these, sees before his eyes the Lamb who redeems with His Blood. The true and blameless Paschal Lamb will be crucified at the very hour when the Mosaic Law required the lambs for the Passover sacrifice to be killed in the Temple and, like the sacrificial lamb, not one of His bones will be broken. (John 19:36; Exodus 12:46). However, Jesus is the triumphant Lamb who, like His ancestor David, defeats all beasts and reptiles and is the heavenly Victor to whom God entrusts the future of the earth. (cf Book of Enoch and Revelation 4).

"He must increase."

Some of John's disciples were upset when they saw that his popularity was giving way to that of Jesus so they went and complained that the Man to whom he had borne witness was now baptising on His own account and everyone was going to Him. This little outbreak of group jealousy was John's opportunity for a final testimony. He explained that he was the Bridegroom's best friend for the wedding soon to be celebrated as Christ gathered His disciples. The best man's duties would conclude with his welcome of the Groom who rejoices in His Bride. (John 3: 22-33).

The comparison would be used again by Jesus in a later discussion about the difference between His attitude and John's. He said he did not deny the value of fasting but the announcement of the Messianic ministry was, like a wedding, a time for celebration. There would be time for mourning when the wedding is interrupted by the Bridegroom's death.

John had said that Jesus must increase as he, himself, decreased. Saint Bede the Venerable noticed that John's birthday was on June 24th when, north of the Tropic of Cancer, the days become shorter while in late December, when Christ is born, they become longer.

After his proclamation of Jesus, John relinquishes the discipleship of Andrew and probably John, the Evangelist to be, with his brother James. Such was the impact of their acceptance of Jesus that they could remember the very moment of their new allegiance, "about the tenth hour". Jesus took them to his home where they stayed the rest of the day and, according to the customs of hospitality, overnight. Andrew collected his brother Simon whom Jesus immediately renames 'Cephas', 'Peter', the rock on which He will build His Church. Philip and Nathaniel (Bartholomew) quickly follow and, generally, John's disciples came to understand more clearly the part he had played as herald and attach themselves to Jesus more readily.

CHAPTER SIX

John lays down his life for his Messiah
(Mark 6:14-29)

Herod Antipas

Herod the Great, BC37-4, who was ruling at the time of Jesus' birth, had a multitude of children by the ladies of his harem and gave his name to at least four of his sons. The one who figures in John's life and death was Herod Antipas, the Tetrarch of Galilee and Peraea, BC4 to 39AD, who, it will be recalled, was reconciled to Pontius Pilate after the mockery of Jesus' trial. When he enters John's story he has already seduced and married Herodias, the wife of his half-brother Herod Philip. She was the daughter of Aristobulus, another of Herod the Great's sons, so her two husbands were also her uncles. By her first marriage she had a daughter, Salome, who later was to emulate her mother's inclination to keep things in the family by marrying an uncle who was Tetrarch of Iturea. Such complicated relationships raised even Roman eyebrows and some confusion about names, even on the part of Evangelists and historians, can easily be forgiven. Herod was superstitious, self-indulgent and proud. He erected public buildings to keep his name alive, like the towns of Sapphoris, four miles from Nazareth, and Tiberias, by the Sea of Galilee, to ingratiate himself with the Emperor Tiberius.

John rebukes Herod and Herodias

Although his Gospel is the shortest, Saint Mark's economic style enables him to relate the episodes in Jesus' life in concise paragraphs. However, the generous space he devotes to the imprisonment and execution of John indicates the importance he attached to his final heroism. As a prophet, John valued highly the functions and responsibilities of royalty. Indeed, his preaching about conversion and change of heart was to prepare for the reign of God in a new Kingdom. He could not ignore the scandalous situation of Herod and Herodias and condemned their adultery in terms unequivocal yet consistent, with a call to repentance and an invitation to receive God's loving forgiveness. Herodias, ambitious, ruthless and in her forties, saw her position threatened by John's intervention and seethed with a profound hatred.

John in prison

Herod had a wary admiration for John whom he recognised as a good and holy man but he was no match for his wife who wanted blood for the reproof. To mollify her, he imprisoned him in the fortress-palace of Machaerus in the Moab mountains east of the Dead Sea. While John was there, Herod consulted him on many issues and listened to him gladly though his motives might have included a wish to impress the Jews that he and his prisoner enjoyed a good working relationship. True, he thought John was a genuine prophet who might have divine powers but he also feared his oratory and popularity could spark a revolt among the people. The vaccilating character was most uncomfortable.

The Good News of the Kingdom

Even in prison, John continued to contribute to the establishing of God's Kingdom. Presumably Herod allowed visits from his disciples because, when they brought him news about Jesus and His activities, he sent them back to ask Him, "Are you the one who is to come?" This seems an odd question because John had already proclaimed Jesus as the Lamb of God and he was no "reed shaken in the wind." He had no doubts at all about who Jesus was but he posed the question for the benefit of his disciples who had not yet folowed the example of Andrew, Peter, James, John, Nathaniel and Philip. Jesus co-operates in the plan and sends them back with news of the miracles which show that the ancient prophecies have come true: "the blind see again, the lame walk, lepers are cleansed, the deaf hear, the dead are raised to life and the Good news is proclaimed to the poor." (Matthew 11: 1ff; Luke 7: 18ff).

The full import of this Messianic declaration by Jesus would have been lost on no one because of familiarity with the prophecy now visibly realised in their own time.

"Look your Lord is coming to you...the eyes of the blind will be opened, the ears of the deaf unsealed, the lame shall leap like a deer and the tongues of the dumb sing for joy...He has sent me to bring good news to the poor, to bind up hearts that are broken, to proclaim liberty to captives, freedom to those in prison and comfort those who mourn." (Isaiah 35: 5-7; 61:1-3). Here is a spiritual reign of charity contrasting with and replacing temporal ostentation and power. With John's encouragement, Jesus has shown how the good news of the Kingdom differs from earlier Jewish expectations. John has preached his baptism of penance to welcome the Kingdom and Jesus shares His good news with everyone through the gifts He brings. God's reign is a revelation of His identity and His Kingdom like a priceless treasure found in a field which changes outlook or an all-embracing net which, cast into the sea, brings home every created fish.

Jesus has brought a spiritual and social reality which gathers all God's family together in His love, mercy and justice. His Church is the sign, sacrament and agent of His Kingdom in this world, continuing His teaching and practice and demonstrating the power and presence of His reign. For all this wonder, John was chosen to make known God's wish that the right conditions in our hearts should be created and our deepest reverence is the natural consequence.

John's martyrdom

Returning to Saint Mark, the time came for Herod's birthday to be celebrated at Machaerus where the palace was a suitable location for a festive banquet. For almost a year he had been unable to make up his mind about John and what course of action would best serve his own personal and political interests. Herodias feared such indecision spelt disaster for her, so she decided to exploit her daughter's charms on a susceptible man. She arranged that, instead of the usual courtesans' dancing for the King, her daughter should do so. Such occasions were not marked by decorum or understatement and the King was so captivated by his step-daughter's performance that he swore to give her anything she wanted, even "half his kingdom", an expression which signified great bounty. At her scheming mother's instigation, Salome asked for John's head to be brought to her on a platter. Herod was horrified. He had a high regard for John, feared the resentment of the Jews, did not enjoy being duped by his wife and royal birthdays were occasions for handing out favours and pardons, not ordering executions. He had been rushed into an act which suited neither his policy nor his inclination but, according to his eccentric conscience, a royal oath could not be broken so he sent guards to kill John. His head is brought to the girl who presents it to her mother.

Saint Mark has recorded a story of corruption, greed, lust, seduction and murder to silence justified condemnation but he takes us beyond the account. John's treatment prefigures that which Jesus will experience in a few years time. Both are arrested and fall into the hands of rulers of weak character despite their temporal power and are executed because of devious and illegal premeditation. The Evangelist is telling us that proclaiming the good news of God's Kingdom and being true to Christian values can be met, not just with apathy, but with devilish hostility.

In modern times, the drama "Salome" was written in French by Oscar Wilde, 1854-1900, and its English translation formed the libretto of the opera by Richard Strauss providing a moving testament to the nobility of our Saint whose martyrdom also bears timely witness to the sanctity of marriage.

Jesus and His disciples mourn John's death

Herod, maybe in a forlorn attempt to stifle remorse, allowed John's disciples to come and collect his body. The tomb, mentioned by Saint Mark and selected for honourable burial, could have been at Sebaste in Samaria. (cf Josephus, 'Antiquities', 18.5.2.). Afterwards, they went to tell Jesus what had transpired and "they all withdrew by boat to a lonely place where they could be by themselves" to mourn their loss.

As so often happened in His life, there was to be no respite for Jesus and soon a large crowd was in hot pursuit. Characteristically, He sympathised with them and chose a moment of profound, personal sadness to cure their ills and give them refreshment. The Baptist's work is done and now a miraculous multiplication of a few loaves and fish is the foretaste of the Eucharistic Banquet. (Matthew 14: 13-21). John's death is a victory and the movement he began was never to be halted as the disciples he prepared for his Messiah proceed to make irreplaceable contributions to the birth and expansion of the Church.

Jesus praises His herald

After John's death, Herod was to hear much more about the mission of Jesus and suspected that this new miracle-worker might be a vengeful Baptist returned to life. Having been warned about the malevolence of the ruler He called "that fox", Jesus withdrew from Galilee and Peraea for a breathing space because the time had not yet come for Him to meet a fate similar to John's. He asked some of the disciples how others

Detail from Dürer's 'Beheading of St John the Baptist'.

perceived Him and was told that some thought He was John and others that He was Elijah or one of the prophets. (Mark 8: 28). In the people's mind Jesus was inseparable from John whom He had always praised and with whom He had associated Himself. In the mystical vision of the Transfiguration when Elijah was recognised by Peter, James and John, they wondered if this was the prophet's return promised by Malachi and if the Kingdom was still awaited. Jesus assured them that it was, indeed, for Elijah to pave the way but that he had already done so in the person of John and, with their deaths, the Old Testament was at an end. As Elijah had been driven to the wilderness by Jezebel's persecution, so John had fallen victim to another Jezebel and Ahab in the persons of Herod and Herodias but he was no waverer swayed by passing breezes on Jordan's banks and his way of life offers a contrast to that of princes, whose pompous progress only disperses and confuses the people.

Jesus took John's example as an opportunity to compare His own generation to capricious children who play music on public festivals and criticise their friends for not joining in. John had proposed an ascetic, monastic ideal but, generally speaking, Palestinian Judaeism did not follow his penitential example and thought his solitary life and appearance signs of madness. When Jesus, on the other hand, offers a moral doctrine without ascetic obligations, He is labelled a drunkard who consorts with all sorts. Human judgment on the one contradicts the verdict on the other and Divine Wisdom is recognised only by those who can accept the complementary messages of Jesus and John.

"The least in the Kingdom."

Whenever Jesus speaks of John it is with an emphasis that demands close attention: "I tell you most solemnly..." John is the last and greatest of the prophets through whom God revealed His intentions and announces the consolation of Israel. He completes the prophetic cycle begun by Elijah in whose spirit "he comes to see that everything is as it should be" and is the first of those martyrs whose sufferings were the birth-pangs of Christianity. His greatness lies, above all, in his recognition of Jesus, the centre of God's Kingdom which surpasses the Old Covenant and fulfils promises beyond imagination. Jesus reminds us that although John was the new Elijah who advanced the day of the Lord, the least in Heaven, the Kingdom of Grace, receives more than the greatest person in this world. Christ has opened the gates of holiness and the channels of grace so that the humblest follower of the Lamb, possessing the gifts of the Gospel dispenstion, outshines all who went before.

CHAPTER SEVEN

Devotion to Saint John the Baptist

The Eastern Church celebrates the Feast of John's Conception on September 23rd and honour him as the Baptiser on January 7th about the time when the Universal Church is recalling the Baptism of the Lord. Obviously, there must have been some strong feeling that God had protected His unique herald and prophet from original sin from the first moment of life, otherwise the celebration of a conception would be inappropriate. It does, however, give some intimation of great devotion to the Saint and the reverence in which he was held. The Western Church was more inclined to believe that the Holy Spirit cleansed John from original sin when, at the Visitation, he leapt for joy in his mother's womb in recognition of the Messiah conceived but yet to born of the Blessed Virgin Mary. Both East and West join in the celebration of his Birthday, therefore, on June 24th and remember his martyrdom (Beheading) on August 29th.

In 362, John's tomb at Sebaste was desecrated by Julian the Apostate, Emperor and nephew of Constantine. His successor, Thedosius the Great, architect of the Catholic Empire housed the precious relics in a magnificent church built in his honour at Alexandria.

John has always been specially honoured by the Monastic Orders who recognise one of their own in his solitary and austere life of prayer, labour and teaching. He enjoyed wide and immense popularity in the middle ages and in England, for example, five hundred churches were dedicated to him, a number exceeded only by those to Our Lady, Saint Peter, Saint Michael and All Saints. Among his many patronages was that of the Knights Hospitallers who undertook the protection of those journeying to and from the Holy Land.

In art, John is represented both as prophet and baptiser and it was as the latter that he found such affection in the hearts of the mediaeval laity. His image appeared frequently in wall-paintings,stained-glass windows, bench ends and statues. He appears dressed in skins, pointing to the Lamb, the 'Agnus Dei', and sometimes carrying a long cross in his other hand as though the age-old prophecies which he completed found their perfection in the Cross of Christ. Significant examples are to be found in York Minster and churches which were associated with the York Cycle of Mystery Plays. Other typical paintings are in the Byward Tower of the Tower of London and the churches at Trimingham, Horsham, Ranworth, Worstead and Attleborough, all in Norfolk. Finally, in fifteenth century Nottingham, there was a thriving industry manufacturing alabaster heads.

John's emblem, the lamb or sometimes a ram, gave mediaeval wool-merchants a feeling of particular affinity with the Saint and they used part of their wealth to build many splendid churches in sheep-country like Norfolk to honour him. It seems churlish to point out that they were grateful for the attractive tax benefits which resulted from their piety and benevolence but it does give some idea of the realm's favourable attitude to worship and those who promoted it.

Saint John the Baptist: the Hymnology

As well as enabling voices to be raised in prayerful song, the concentrated beauty and meaning of inspired poetry are aids to personal prayer and meditation. With such a hope are some examples offered.

The great forerunner of the morn,
The herald of the Word is born;
And faithful hearts shall never fail
With thanks and praise his light to hail.

With heavenly message Gabriel came,
That John should be that herald's name,
And, with prophetic utterance, told
His actions great and manifold.

John, still unborn, yet gave aright
His witness to the coming Light;
And Christ, the Sun of all the earth,
Fulfilled that witness at his birth.

Of woman-born shall never be
A greater prophet than was he,
Whose mighty deed exalt his fame
To greater than a prophet's name.

(St Bede the Venerable, 673-735. Tr. J.M.Neale, 1818-66).

ST JOHN THE BAPTIST

Sing we the praises of the great forerunner,
Tell forth the mighty wonders of his story;
So make his Master cleanse our lips and make them
Fit to extol him.

Lo, God's high herald, swift from heaven descending,
Gives to thy father tidings of thy coming,
Telling thy name and all the tale of marvels
That shall befall thee.

Oft had the prophets in the tome before thee
Spoken in vision of the Daystar's coming;
But when He came, 'twas thou that didst proclaim
Him Saviour of all men.

(Paul the Deacon, 8th Century).

God called His prophets to foretell
The coming of his Son;
The greatest, called before his birth,
Was John, the chosen one.

John searched in solitude for Christ
And knew Him when He came.
He showed the world the Lamb of God
And hailed Him in our name.

That lonely voice cried out the truth,
Derided and denied.
As witness to the Law of God
His mighty martyr died.

(Liturgy of the Hours, June 24th).

ST JOHN THE BAPTIST

O sylvan prophet, whose eternal fame
Resounds from Jewry's hills and Jordan's streams,
The music of our numbers raise
And tune our voice to sing thy praise.

Heaven's messenger from high Olympus came
To bear the tidings of thy life and name,
And told thy sire each prodigy
That Heaven designed to work in thee.

He heard the news and dubious with surprise,
His faltering speech in fettered accents dies;
But Providence with happy choice
In thee restored thy father's voice.

From the recess of nature's inmost room,
Thou knew'st thy Lord unborn from womb to womb,
Whilst each glad parent told and blest
The secrets of each other's breast.

Glory to God the Father and the Son,
And Holy Ghost, with both in nature one,
Whose equal power unites the three
In one eternal Trinity.

(John Dryden, 1631-1701).

Sources and References

Introducing the New Testament.
John Drane. Lion Publishing, 1986.

Catholic Commentary on the Holy Scripture.
Thomas Nelson and Sons, 1951.

Commentary on the Bible,
Matthew Henry. Harper Collins, 1960.

Catechism of the Catholic Church.
Geoffrey Chapman, 1994.

Cambridge Companion to the Bible.
Cambridge University Press, 1997.

Bible Alive.
Bible Alive Ltd.

The Jerusalem Bible.
Darton, Longman and Todd Ltd, 1974.

The Divine Office.
Collins, 1974.